JUNIOR BIOGRAPHIES

EMMA STONE

ACTRESS

Enslow Publishing
101 W. 23rd Street
Suite 240
New York, NY 10011
USA

enslow.com

Therese M. Shea

WORDS TO KNOW

anxiety Fear about what might happen.

asthma A physical condition that makes it difficult for someone to breathe.

audition To try out for a role.

charity An organization that helps people who are poor, sick, or in need.

debut The first time an actor does something in public.

nomination The act of choosing someone as the possible winner of an award.

tattoo A picture or word that is permanently drawn on a person's skin by using a needle and ink.

therapist A person who helps people deal with mental or emotional problems by talking about those problems.

CONTENTS

Emma Stone

Emma Stone's movie career began early. She was just a teenager when she had her first big role. She was not an overnight star, though. Emma had to work hard to find roles at first. However, once she got her break, she was quickly noticed, earning **nominations** for major awards. Today, Emma is one of the most in-demand actors in the world!

EARLY DAYS

Emma Stone was born Emily Jean Stone in Scottsdale, Arizona, on November 6, 1988. She has one younger brother named Spencer. For the first six months of her life, Emma had a condition called colic. She cried so

Emma found out she had **asthma** on the set of the 2010 movie *Easy A*.

Emma is close with her brother Spencer, who is two years younger than she is.

much that she hurt her vocal cords. Emma still loses her voice easily today because of this.

A DIFFICULT TIME

As a young girl, Emma suffered from panic attacks. Her chest would feel tight, and she would have a hard time breathing. She was so worried that something bad was going to happen to her that she stopped going to friends' houses.

Emma Says:

"You can't afford to think about a million other things [when you're acting]. You have to think about the task at hand."

Even going to school was difficult. She remembers visiting the school nurse on most days.

Emma began seeing a **therapist**, which helped with her **anxiety**. However, she said it was taking part in theater that really helped her overcome her problem. She started acting at the age of eleven. She was so busy thinking about what she would say or do next on stage that she had little time to worry about anything else.

Chapter 2
A Major Move

Emma began high school in 2003. After a half year, she decided she wanted to move to Los Angeles, California, to start an acting career there. But first, she had to convince her parents that it was a good idea. She put her computer skills to use.

Project Hollywood

Emma had been interested in computers from a young age. She even published her own e-newsletter. Emma used her talents to create a computer presentation that she called "Project Hollywood." She included music in the background—a song by Madonna called "Hollywood."

Emma Says:

"I think my ultimate goal at the end of the day is to make my parents laugh . . . just like I did in the living room when I was a kid."

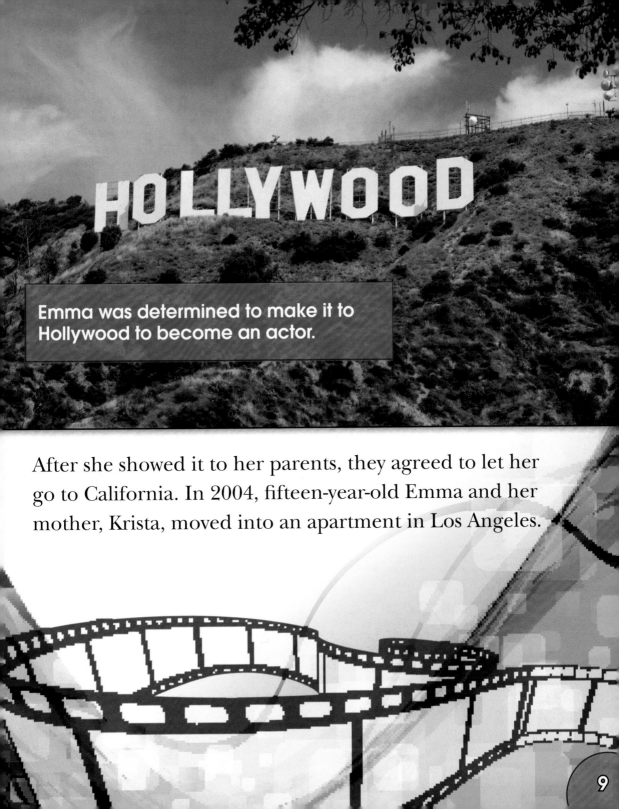

Emma was determined to make it to Hollywood to become an actor.

After she showed it to her parents, they agreed to let her go to California. In 2004, fifteen-year-old Emma and her mother, Krista, moved into an apartment in Los Angeles.

As a teenager, Emma enjoyed her early success in Los Angeles.

Emma worked at a dog bakery while she was waiting for her big break in Los Angeles.

IN SEARCH OF FAME

Emma's first break was in reality television. A 2004 VH1 show called *In Search of the New Partridge Family* was a contest in which young actors competed for a role on a television show. Emma sang the song "We Belong" by Pat Benatar. The audience loved her—she won! The show was never made, however.

With the help of a manager, Emma landed some small roles on other television shows. She also **auditioned** for a lead in the show *Heroes*. She was very disappointed when she did not get the part. She called losing that role "rock bottom."

CHAPTER 3
THE BIG BREAK AND BEYOND

In 2007, Emma made her film **debut** in the teen movie *Superbad*. The hit led to more roles in comedies, including *The Rocker*, *The House Bunny*, *Ghost of Girlfriends Past*, and *Zombieland*.

In 2010, Emma starred in the comedy *Easy A*. It was based on the novel *The Scarlet Letter* by Nathaniel Hawthorne. Emma was nominated for a Golden Globe Award for Best Actress for her performance as a high school student.

In 2011, Emma was praised again for her role in the movie *The Help*. She played an author in the 1960s who interviews African American maids about their experiences working for white families.

Emma Says:

"I did *Superbad* in what would've been my senior year. I was playing a senior, and had I graduated I would've missed that opportunity, and had I missed that opportunity I wouldn't be here right now."

Emma attends the premiere of her movie *Easy A* in 2010.

A RANGE OF ROLES

Next, Emma played Peter Parker's girlfriend, Gwen Stacy, in the superhero movies *The Amazing Spider-Man* (2012) and *The Amazing Spider-Man 2* (2014) alongside Andrew Garfield.

But Emma was also offered more serious parts and excelled at them. She took a role in the movie *Birdman or (The Unexpected Virtue of Ignorance)* in 2014. She played a recovering drug addict who was the daughter of a

Ryan Gosling costarred with Emma in *Crazy, Stupid, Love.*

Birdman or (The Unexpected Virtue of Ignorance) won the Oscar for Best Picture in 2015.

Hollywood star. She was nominated for an Oscar for Best Supporting Actress for this role.

Emma took a break from the movies in 2014, but not from acting. She performed as nightclub singer Sally Bowles in *Cabaret* on Broadway in New York City for three months.

HOLLYWOOD MUSICAL

It was Emma's role in *Cabaret*—and her singing and dancing—that got the attention of director Damien

When Emma Stone accepted her Oscar, she said, "I still have a lot of growing and learning and work to do, and this (award) is a really beautiful symbol to continue on that journey, and I'm so grateful for that."

Chazelle. He was looking for a lead for his next movie, a musical called *La La Land*. He asked Emma to play Mia, a young woman hoping to break into the movie business. She falls in love with a jazz pianist named Sebastian, played by Ryan Gosling, who is pursuing his dream of opening a jazz club.

Both Gosling and Stone had to sing and dance in their roles. Emma won many honors for her part, including a Golden Globe Award and the Oscar for Best Actress in 2017.

CHAPTER 4
EMMA'S INTERESTS

Emma has many interests outside of acting. One is working with charities that help fight cancer. Emma's mother, Krista, found out she had cancer when Emma was nineteen. Emma flew home to Arizona often to be with her while she was undergoing treatments. Her mother is now cancer-free, but Emma still helps support organizations that help others with the disease, such as Gilda's Club and Stand Up To Cancer.

Emma and her mother Krista got matching tattoos of blackbirds to celebrate her beating cancer.

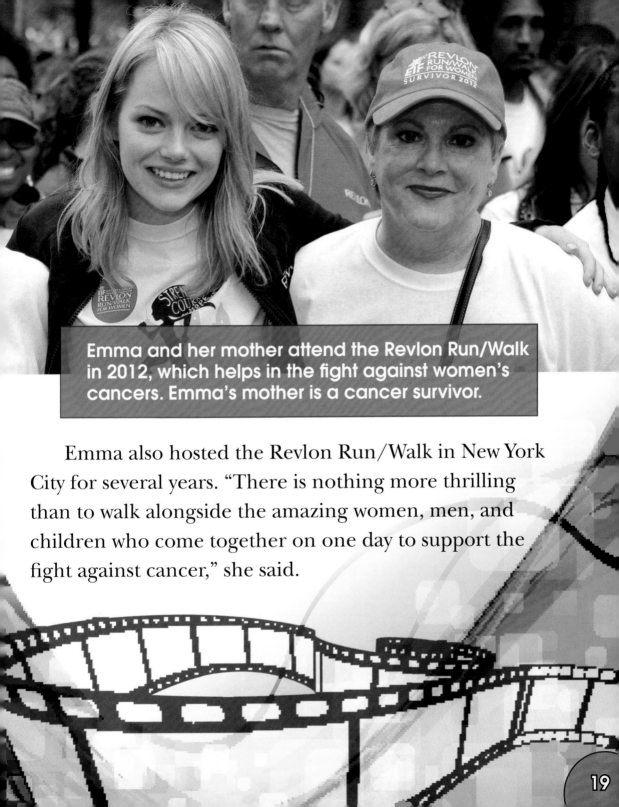

Emma and her mother attend the Revlon Run/Walk in 2012, which helps in the fight against women's cancers. Emma's mother is a cancer survivor.

Emma also hosted the Revlon Run/Walk in New York City for several years. "There is nothing more thrilling than to walk alongside the amazing women, men, and children who come together on one day to support the fight against cancer," she said.

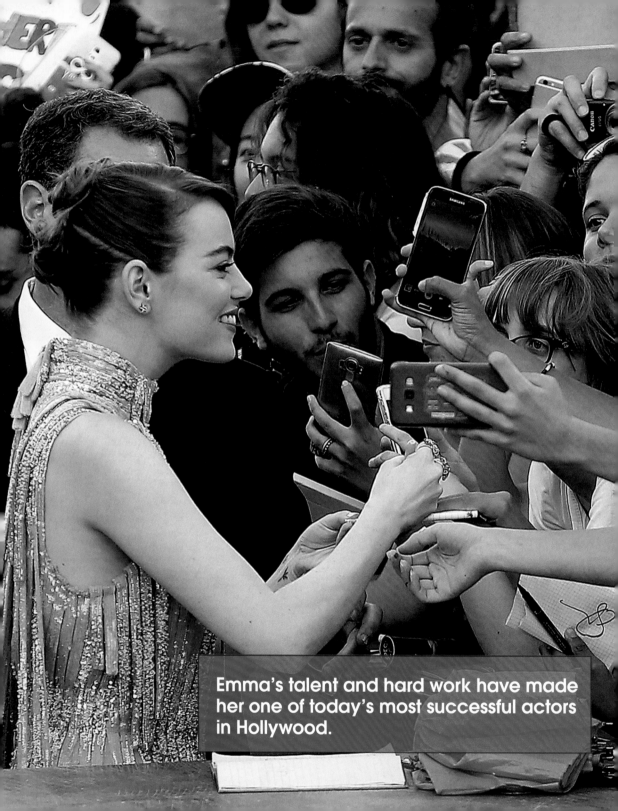

Emma's talent and hard work have made her one of today's most successful actors in Hollywood.

Emma has also taken part in **charity** work for Earth Hour, which organizes events to fight climate change, as well as other groups that help people in need.

RISING STAR

Emma is now one of the highest-paid actresses in the world. She does not like to talk about her private life. However, people are drawn to her because she seems like the "girl next door" rather than a major movie star. She credits her family for keeping her down to earth.

Emma wants to keep testing her talents in new kinds of roles. What will this Oscar winner do next?

Emma Says:

"I always thought it was more important to be funny or honest than to look a certain way."

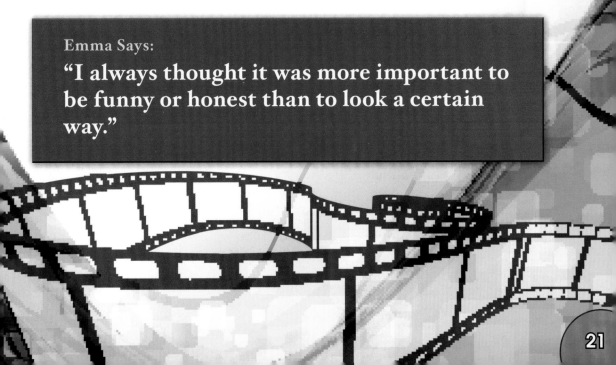

1988 Emily Jean (Emma) Stone is born in Scottsdale, Arizona, on November 6.

1999 Begins acting in local theater productions.

2004 Moves with her mother to Los Angeles, California.

2004 Wins the reality TV competition *In Search of the New Partridge Family.*

2007 Makes her film debut in the movie *Superbad.*

2010 Plays the starring role in the comedy *Easy A.*

2011 Wins praise for her part as an author in the movie *The Help.*

2014 Is nominated for an Oscar for Best Supporting Actress for her role in *Birdman or (The Unexpected Virtue of Ignorance)*. Stars in *Cabaret* on Broadway.

2017 Wins the Best Actress Oscar for her role in *La La Land.*

BOOKS

Schuman, Michael A. *Emma! Amazing Actress Emma Stone.* Berkeley Heights, NJ: Enslow Publishers, 2013.

Spence, Kelly. *Emma Stone.* New York, NY: Crabtree Publishing Company, 2015.

Tieck, Sarah. *Emma Stone: Talented Actress.* Minneapolis, MN: ABDO Publishing, 2013.

WEBSITES

Emma Stone
www.biography.com/people/emma-stone-20874773
Read a short biography of the actress's life.

Emma Stone Web
www.emmastoneweb.com
Get the latest news, interviews, articles, and photos of Emma.

Index

Published in 2019 by Enslow Publishing, LLC.
101 W. 23rd Street, Suite 240, New York, NY 10011

Library of Congress Cataloging-in-Publication Data
Names: Shea, Therese author.
Title: Emma Stone : actress / Therese M. Shea.
Description: New York : Enslow Publishing, 2019. | Series: Junior biographies
 | Includes bibliographical references and index. | Audience: Grades 3-6.
Identifiers: LCCN 2017044742| ISBN 9780766097315 (library bound) | ISBN
 9780766097322 (pbk.) | ISBN 9780766097339 (6 pack)
Subjects: LCSH: Stone, Emma, 1988–Juvenile literature. | Actors–United
 States–Biography–Juvenile literature.
Classification: LCC PN2287.S73 S44 2017 | DDC 791.4302/8092 [B] –dc23
LC record available at https://lccn.loc.gov/2017044742

Printed in the United States of America

To Our Readers: We have done our best to make sure all website addresses in this book were active and appropriate when we went to press. However, the author and the publisher have no control over and assume no liability for the material available on those websites or on any websites they may link to. Any comments or suggestions can be sent by e-mail to customerservice@enslow.com.

Photo Credits: Cover, p. 1 Jason LaVeris/FilmMagic/Getty Images; p. 4 Jeff Kravitz/FilmMagic/Getty Images; p. 6 Gregg DeGuire/FilmMagic/Getty Images; p. 9 Kirk Wester/Shutterstock.com; p. 10 Mirek Towski/FilmMagic/Getty Images; p. 13 Philip Ramey Photography, LLC/Corbis Entertainment/Getty Images; p. 14 Pictorial Press Ltd/Alamy Stock Photo; p. 16 Kevin Winter/Getty Images; p. 19 Stephen Lovekin/WireImage/Getty Images; p. 20 Danny Martindale/FilmMagic/Getty Images; interior page bottoms (celluloid film strip) Alena Kazlouskaya/Shutterstock.com.